THE LONG HAUL

Alan Buckley

HAPPENSTANCE

Poems © Alan Buckley, 2016
Cover image © Gillian Rose, 2016
ISBN 978-1-910131-28-2
All rights reserved

ACKNOWLEDGMENTS:

Versions of some of these poems first appeared in the following magazines and anthologies: *Ambit, Cake, The Dark Horse, Oxford Poetry* and *The Rialto; Days of Roses II, Double Bill, Hand Luggage Only, Live Canon 2015* and *Map: Poems After William Smith's Geological Map of 1815*.

'Sherbet Lemons' and 'Being a Beautiful Woman' were highly commended in the 2012 and 2014 Bridport Prizes.

'Voicemail' won the Wigtown Poetry Competition in 2010.

The middle section of 'Dovey Junction' quotes from Chapter Six of Alexander Frater's 1983 book *Stopping Train Britain*.

'Found' is based on the words of Trevor Saunders, who discovered the body of Gemma Adams. He was quoted in the article 'Dead bodies: people who find corpses and body parts', written by Julie Bindel and published in *The Guardian* 25/07/09.

Thanks are due to Andy Ching, Paul Farley, John Glenday, Jen Hadfield, The Thurlow Road Group and Ben Wilkinson for their comments on earlier drafts of these poems. Particular thanks to Helen Mort for all her advice and encouragement.

Printed by The Dolphin Press
www.dolphinpress.co.uk

Published in 2016 by HappenStance,
21 Hatton Green, Glenrothes, Fife KY7 4SD
nell@happenstancepress.com
www.happenstancepress.com

CONTENTS

Flame / 5
Loch Ness / 6
Sherbet Lemons / 7
Being a Beautiful Woman / 8
Psychotherapy / 10
Pastoral / 11
Mr and Mrs Clark and Percy / 12
His Failure / 13
Red Rock / 14
The Unchosen / 15
Stalactites / 16
Little Machine / 18
Haunts / 19
Dovey Junction / 20
Found / 22
The Alchemist / 23
The Line / 24
Voicemail / 27
Gravity / 28

FLAME

Use matches sparingly
　　—instruction on front of matchbox

Not meanness or thrift
but wisdom; respect
for each small torch
that's kept in there. Lover,

the same is true for words.
I bring you no fireworks.
A room is never so dark
that it needs more

than one slim burst
of sulphur to show
the mirror hung on its wall,
the way to its door.

And lovers know too
how even a single
flame might raise
a scar that time can't heal.

So come, stand next to me;
let's flip this little box.
Strike softly away from body.
See how it urges us.

LOCH NESS

The man who told me swears this is true.
That first summer after the war, his father,
cycling at dusk near Invermoriston,
came across it beached on the road.
Near-dead—limp-lipped, the scales already dulled—
but still some crazy glimmer in its eyes
as if it had dragged itself from the loch
to prove it did exist. He summoned help.

They dug a trench, then pitched the monster in
and buried it. These people had faith
and knew how a distant log, drawn strangely
by the water's undertow, might feed
the mind's eye better than the thing itself.
And who'd come more than once to see
a rotting fish? Better, surely, to have
the doubt, the ache of possibility.

SHERBET LEMONS

Out of reach, high
in a wall of glass jars.
The newsagent clambers
up steps. Bitter pearls,

rattled onto scales, slid
into a white paper bag.
I feel their stickiness,
hold one up to the light.

It glowers back, a sour
eye. The shine defies
my milky teeth: I work
my tongue, slither

and roll, until the shell
relents with a crack.
A startle of yellow fizz:
I think of her, late at night

in a room I'll never see,
unleashing that shock
of blonde. How it shivers
down her naked back.

BEING A BEAUTIFUL WOMAN

is like owning a dog. A dangerous
dog—one of those breeds the papers
go on about. Pit Bull. Rottweiler.

You take your dog for a walk,
and crowds part in front of you,
as if under some kind of spell.

Some people won't come near you.
They stand at a distance, hands
in pockets, stare at your dog.

Others make a big show of being
fearless. They stroke your dog
forcefully, speak to it too loudly.

If people talk to *you*, it's usually
about your dog. Some have dogs
themselves. Or wish that they did.

You long to set your dog free,
for it to run around the park and lick
and dig and shit as it pleases.

But all your life you've been told
how lucky you are to own this dog.
It's criminal to neglect it.

You have to feed your dog with choice
cuts of meat, groom it, pamper it,
make it the centre of your world.

Above all else, you have to keep it
on a short leash. It's your fault
if somebody dies because of it.

PSYCHOTHERAPY

Summer of '86. Still a student, before
the wilderness years of my twenties,
the groping towards a career,
and me and a friend had blagged our way
to New York. We saw them perform
off-Broadway: Penn all spiel and patter,
Teller his mute sidekick. Back then
it was novel, deconstructing magic
in front of an audience. To close the show
Penn delivered a monologue on eating fire.
How d'you not burn your mouth?—
that was what people always asked him

and his big reveal was this: there is
no trick. You do burn your mouth,
especially to begin with. What's more,
each time you do the act you swallow
some lighter fluid. It makes you nauseous,
slowly poisons your liver. No matter:
his explanation just deepened my sense
of wonder. He paused, as if to gather
his thoughts, then shifted his gaze, and I swear
his eyes were focussed on mine. *Magic
is fake. Sideshow skills are real. You shouldn't
ask how we're doing this, but why.*

PASTORAL

Glimpsed for no more than a second or two
(I was pushing eighty-five near Stokenchurch Gap)
but enough for a thought to surface: the possibility

that the heft of snout and fur by the central barrier
belonged to a creature that was deaf and asleep,
having nodded off in the morning sun as it looked

for a chance to cross; and this was why it lay there,
oblivious to the cars and lorries bouldering past.
Deaf and asleep, its belly filled with a slither

of worms as it dreamed its brockish dreams,
in which it was busy reliving the night just gone,
when it scuttled through fields of silvery grass

beneath an avuncular moon. And beyond the black,
hard river that carves its way down Aston Hill
a hole in the earth was waiting—a small darkness,

ready to fall back behind this animal's tail, like
the heavy curtain at the entrance to a private room,
shielding from view a silent, untouchable space.

MR AND MRS CLARK AND PERCY

David Hockney, 1970-71, acrylic paint on canvas

I like the way you capture that chic milieu—
Ossie's chrome-frame chair, the white telephone
casually untabled on the carpet, Celia's
purple smock dress. And I like how I'm shown
too much, the genre subverted: husband seated,
not wife; no flow of gaze from one to the other
to viewer, but both facing me from either
side of the window's gulf. I'm made complicit,
a triangle's third point. But what I love is the cat,
Blanche given Percy's name; you decided that
was artistically correct. Back turned to me it sits,
slender and erect, on Ossie's faithless lap,
staring out at something beyond all this
deceit, at something beyond my grasp.

HIS FAILURE

December 31st. Almost a year without cigarettes.
Fear of death had done the trick. At the party, I met
Elena: she smiled, and the gap between her front teeth
only made her more beautiful. She offered me
a Marlboro Light, then lifted her foot, struck a match
off the scuffing on the sole of her black
stiletto. I tell you, I pulled so hard on that filter
I nearly sucked in the whole damn universe. I felt
like a god. No—scrub the indefinite article—
like God. My hangover, though, was two days of hell.

But no regrets. To fall just short of perfection
is to leave a necessary space. Take the temptation
of Gawain, how in the end Bertilak's foxy lady
got him, despite his chivalric codes and priggish piety.
He came back all boo-hoo and tail between his legs,
her bright green girdle slung over that nick on his neck,
and crazy with shame—he heard Camelot's laughter
as a monstrous choir, confirming his failure.
Didn't get it, how they truly welcomed him home;
welcomed him, finally, as one of their own.

RED ROCK

Thor's Stone on Thurstaston Common, once thought to be
an ancient man-made feature, is either a glacial erratic,
or a product of weathering of the hill's bedrock.
   — Martin Amlot, 'A History of Thurstaston'

My mind's unsure, but my legs
carry their own memory. I stride
through birch, rowan, oak, step out
into the clearing, its banks purple
with heather-bell, ling. I climb the rock,
and it's easier and harder than before,
my adult shoes too big for the grooves
and gullies. The top's a memorial,
names and hearts roughly carved:
at one end a scorched hollow, frilled
with ash; in it a winded tinnie, a gasless
lighter, the roach of a joint, sucked brown.
Some claim Norsemen made sacrifices
here, though the rock dwarfs all stories;
it is its own myth. I've come back
to this jut of land that rises between
Dee and Mersey, and I know it's not where
I was born, and it's not where I've lived
for thirty years. But knowing is half a lie.
Here—a knuckle of this peninsula's spine:
there's red in my veins, red beneath my feet,
and today, at least, I feel where I stand.

THE UNCHOSEN

I meet a former lover
in a bright café. We sip coffee,

try not to breathe
too deeply, and hug so only

our upper bodies touch.
There are others in the space

between us whom we must lean
over—the ones, we assume,

who came later, the wiser,
kindlier lovers. But if we chose

to look down we'd see instead
the children we once refused

staring up at us, their half-
familiar eyes filled with something

that might be judgement
or might be sorrow.

STALACTITES

Underneath Sharpham House, Devon

We're born of water's yearning
to find its way home. We hang,
lime mortar's weeping,
through decade on decade.
This cellar's both womb and world.
We don't need the fickle sun,
the wayward moon. We hear
your brief passing—the precision
of heels on stone; a stomp of boots,
the floorboards' protesting creak.
And voices, trying to make
this house their own. Silence,
though, is a sitting tenant.
Most of you offer your words
to the sky, pray to be seen.
But what could the infinite
recognise in you? A few,
like yourself, have the sense
to walk down those steps,
waving a torch like a charm
before them. A sharp inhale:
here's commitment, a vision
of small eternities framed
by arches of unglazed brick,
rusting pipes, a dirt floor.

Here's a cathedral that praises
the imperceptible, dressed
in immaculate white.
Come, put your faith in us.
We'll show you what it means
to be in it for the long haul.

LITTLE MACHINE

i.m. JHB

They say that talent skips a generation,
and you'd have agreed, looking at me, your son.
You who were happy grappling under a bonnet,
as deft at the wrench as the fine adjustment,
while I fumbled with a long screwdriver
trying to lever off a bicycle tyre.
The punctured inner tube was left more wounded.
The lunge of your blunt words: me, marooned
in a silence that no gauge could measure,
you with a face like a man in a seizure.
I sloped off, back to my exercise books
full of poems, long-handed in cursive loops.

I abandoned them, hid them up in the attic,
my teenage world flipped by girls and music.
You said, years later—I'd not long turned thirty—
how, as a kid, you'd wanted to write poetry,
how the tireless grip of your mother's cold stare
stopped you dead, and I felt something stir,
a tick, or a pulse. You see, I've still no craft
with lathes, micrometers, drills. Here's my gift.
Listen to these words, their fit and throw,
this little machine that is breathing you,
its chittering valves and burnished tappets,
the cams in their endless, elliptical dance.

HAUNTS

for Nomi and Lyra

This is the city where you
gave birth to her perfect stillness,
held her, let her go. So now
you have to leave—it's too much
to bear: I imagine there's a ghost
of you, still heavy with her, that walks
along the streets you walk,
soft-footed, griefless.

But I'm wrong, you say. This
is the ghost life; it's me who's haunting
the other. Night comes. That full-bellied
woman glances through a window,
startles. She soothes herself—
just a trick of the glass—then turns
away. I'm left outside staring in,
and only the darkness can hold me.

DOVEY JUNCTION

There are worse lives I might have led
than his, witness to the seasons' slow
shift—cotton grass, yellow flag,
bog myrtle, bulrush; osprey, nightjar,
darter, snipe. Here the river parts its lips
to speak an estuary, the rails divide,
and he's monarch of the marsh,
signals in three counties drop their arms
at his bidding. Block bells *ting-ting*
(train entering section: up stopping
from Aber). Reeds waver, salmon glint

then vanish. A constant lapping
of water, *Laver's Liverpool Tide Tables*
always to hand—he remembers
that January night: *A roar in the west,
then half the Irish Sea fell out of the sky.
I saw the Gents go under like a U-boat
venting its tanks; 'Put your coat on Hughes,'
I said, 'it's time to go home.' On my hands
and knees I was, sleeper to sleeper,
pulling myself along the rails, waves
breaking about my ears—it was like
Waikiki beach out there.*

I've been that man myself, of course,
stunned, bedraggled, wondering how
I'd survived the arrival of love. I've stared
at the wreckage, believing the flood

came out of the blue. But that's a lie:
wherever it was I crawled to for safety,
it's my heart that roared, my heart
the waters rose from.

FOUND

On the first anniversary I planted a buddleia
here on the bank. I come here every day.
I feel I know her; there's a bond between us.

I keep asking myself *What makes a person do
a thing like that?* But I'm glad I found her.
It made the police start looking for the others.

And from that moment, I felt she was at peace.
The following night, I dreamt we were both
by the brook. She turned to me, said *Thank you*.

I noticed something alien protruding
from the water. I thought it was a mannequin.
I touched the shape; it was freezing cold.

As I cleared away the leaves and debris
a globule of congealed blood drifted past.
The body was on its front, arms outstretched.

I uncovered the head. Her face was on its side;
her eyes were open. She just looked like a normal
person. I'd been checking for flood damage;

it was unusually sunny for the time of year.
I remember thinking how pleasant it was
to hear the birds singing after days of rain.

THE ALCHEMIST

The four-year-old boy knows the joy of it,
though he doesn't understand how it happens,
as he runs, snugged up in a duffle coat
on the sandstone ridge between
the windmill and the observatory,
pretending to be one of those trains—
woofing a trail of clouds behind it—
that's recently vanished from his world.
He sees his breath hang in winter's brightness.

He never gets bored of this casual alchemy,
the unseen made visible, something outside him
taken into his body, changed, and then
let go; a swirl of mist that's him
and not him intermingled. Though this
isn't what the boy's thinking. He's remembering
a big black engine, its warm oil smell,
as I am now. We stand wide-eyed,
each printing his ghost on the generous air.

THE LINE

There is a border, with love on one side and madness on the other.
But only God can see it
    —Arabic proverb

Waiting for the lock at Somerton Deep
I end up chatting with the old boy moored
in front. Knew the cut as it used to be,
a proper working canal. He tells the story
of Harry Jacks—a coal-boat man, and far
from the quickest one, but not through laziness
or lack of skill. A man obsessed with the line:
that thread, invisible to most,
by which a narrowboat's guided through
each bend and rabbit-hole bridge
with just the required steer, no more.

The way he'd stand on the stern—leaning
forward, one eye screwed up tight—as if
he imagined himself in Brindley's shoes,
two centuries before: looking through
his theodolite, and gauging the easiest route
to build that hugged the contours close.
Some men sheared their tiller bars, racing
the cut's tight loops round Wormleighton Hill.
Not Harry, who held that length of brass
like a lover's arm, carried to greet the dance.

His reputation grew. A lad from Aynho way
became, in turn, as fixed on the line
as Harry himself. One day he looped
up cradles out of twine, a duck egg

in each one. He brought them here to the lock,
and dangled them down the chamber walls
as Harry came up from the south.
Picture it—a sixty-foot steel hull, the gap
no bigger than the width of a hand each side . . .

What if the lad and the old boy were one
and the same? It would add a nice touch
to this story, certainly. Either way,
now the gates swing back, a prow nods out:
the old boy's turn to move. Or he and I
are caught in a burst of rain, and stumble
off to our boats for jackets and caps.

Believe me, it doesn't matter. Look—
there's a lock called Somerton Deep, for sure.
And once I talked with someone I'd met there.
But spin the clock back far enough
and there's no brick-lined cavity,
its walls made green with weed;
no surveyor has come this way, no gang
of navvies with spades. Go further still,
and there's no Leonardo, Vinci's famous son,
envisaging canals that climb up hills.
The mitred gates that will master
the water's flow haven't yet been sketched.
Not even a thought is there.

All that exists is all there's ever been,
an aching geometry, that shapes

our journey whether we know it or not.
And as for Harry Jacks, he's as real
as we need him to be. Already you've seen
his boat gone past, its perfect line,
and a kid with coal-glint eyes and fiery hands
holding the eggs intact.

VOICEMAIL

for Kate

Although your mobile must be lying still
and unblinking on a bedside table

or stuffed in a bag with a pointless diary,
tonight I ring it one last time and hear

your voice, clear, unwavering, as you ask me
to *please leave a message after the tone*

and then I try to pretend you're busy,
writing songs on your scuffed acoustic, or down

in the lush, quiet county where you were born,
hands on the steering wheel's leopard-print cover,

casually speeding south through a warren
of hedge-bound lanes, stone bridges, up over

Eggardon Hill, to the place you'd go to stare
at the waves, breathe the incoming air.

GRAVITY

The aerialist swings out, hair rippling,
beyond the proscenium arch. Just below
the dead point, where upward force
and downward pull are perfectly matched,
she lets go—we gasp—of the *corde volante*,
and there, for a heartbeat, body and rope
are floating apart. Later, she'll smile:
*Whatever you choose to think, I cannot fly. I fall
professionally.* But the woman above us now
is not the one with tied-back hair, calloused
hands, who carefully checks the shackles
and silks before the audience comes. She
has vanished, as we all have, briefly released
from our fragile, desperate weight.